THE REVERSE COLORING BOOK™

MINDFUL JOURNEYS

Kendra Norton

Workman Publishing
New York

T0382848

REVERSE COLORING IDEAS

Not sure where to start? Try some of these ideas and see where they take you!

Thick lines

thin lines

fast

doodles

hearts

Tiny Patterns

Stacking shapes

Whimsy

PATTERNS

Circles

hamsa

Mandala

Leaves

waves

double lines

Single LINES

Lotus

flowers

illustrations

THERE ARE NO RULES! You can use any pen you like. I use felt-tip, non-bleeding, permanent ink pens. They look similar to the one depicted on the cover. They come in a variety of sizes and colors. Experiment with a few to see what you love best!

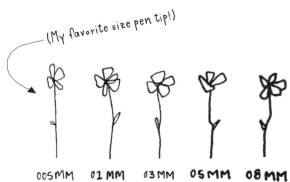

(My favorite size pen tip!)

005MM   01MM   03MM   05MM   08MM

*"This is a wonderful day.
I've never seen this one before."
—Maya Angelou*

Welcome to the third in the Reverse Coloring Book series—*Mindful Journeys*!

You'll notice each of these paintings is imperfectly perfect—an invitation to let go of all the expectations of artistry you may have. You can fill the book with lines and meditative patterns—or whatever you want. Most important is to allow space for all the beautiful imperfections that come when we engage in art, in life, in each of our own mindful journeys.

What if you decide to allow every moment you spend drawing to be okay—exactly as it is. When thoughts get in the way, try slowing down; focus on the small details or patterns or the way you are breathing. Release any ideas you may have about how it all *should* be . . . and just keep going. This book can unlock a whole new avenue for mindfulness and meditation—one where your progress can be seen and celebrated on paper. Your very own creative, mindful journey.

You can create worlds within worlds—in your spirit, and in your drawing!

With love, always,

Kendra Norton

P.S. Please keep sharing your pages on Instagram and Tiktok @Kendranortonart. I love collaborating with you. ♥

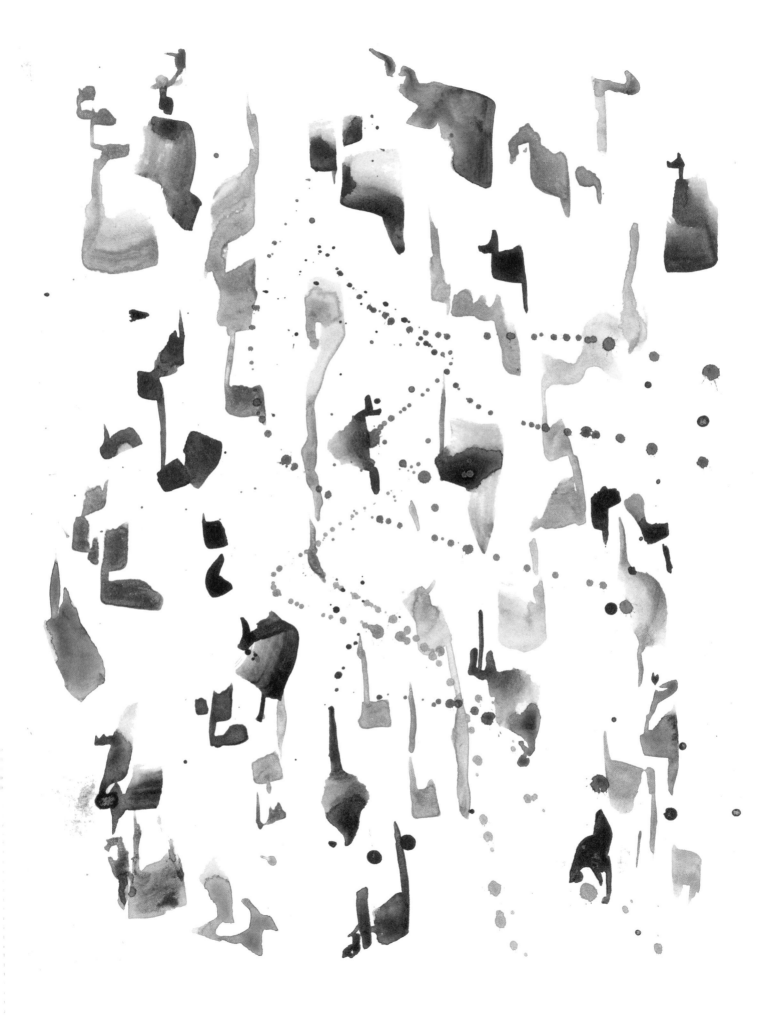

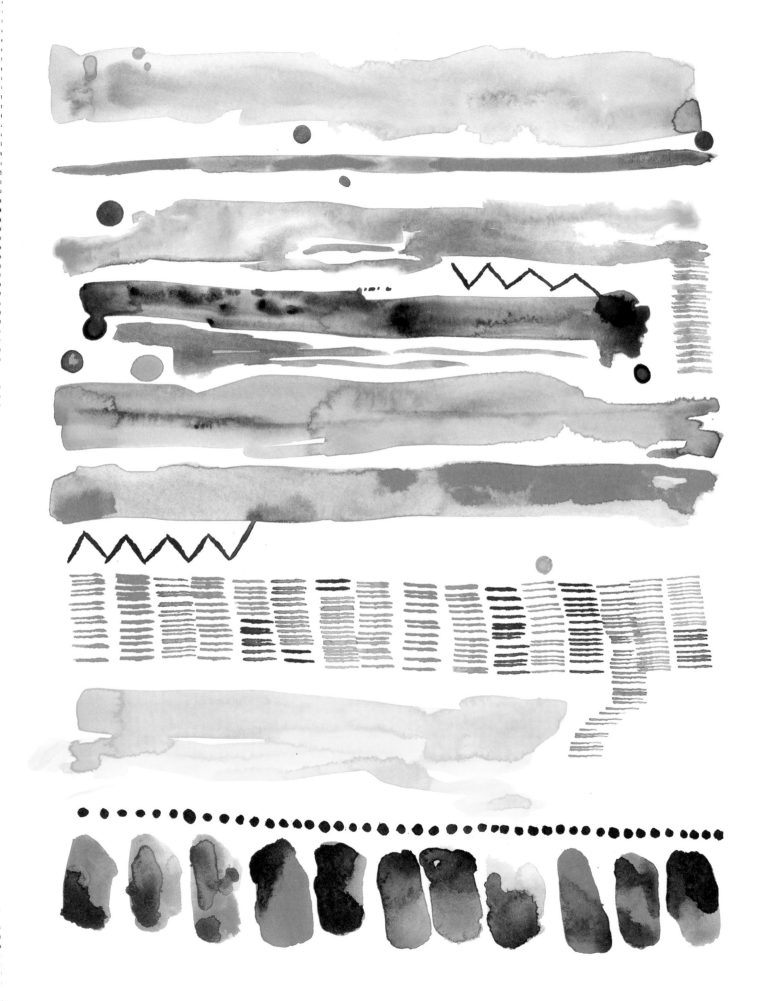

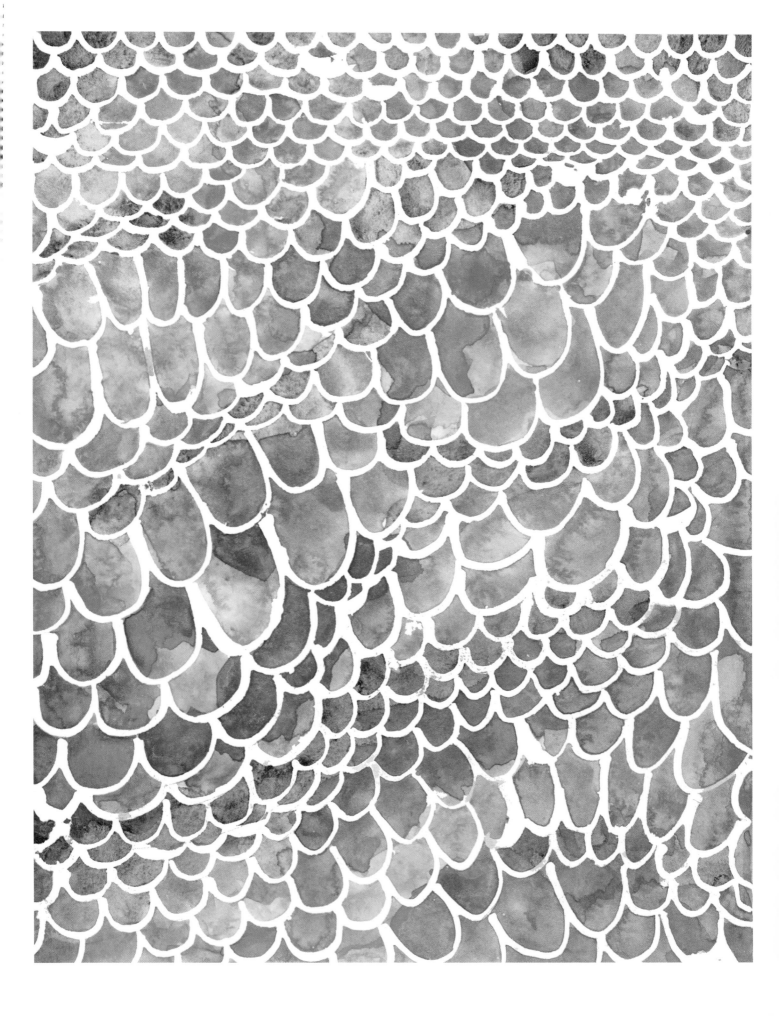

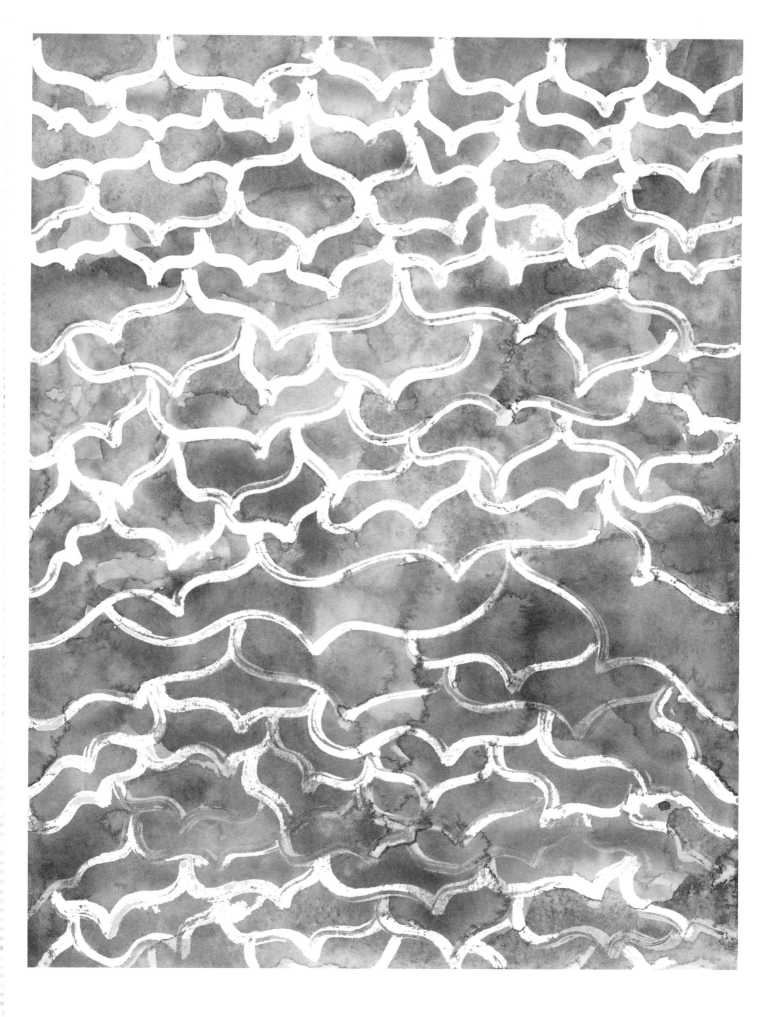

Workman
Workman Publishing
Hachette Book Group, Inc.
1290 Avenue of the Americas
New York, NY 10104
workman.com

THE REVERSE COLORING BOOK is a trademark of Kendra Norton.

Workman is an imprint of Workman Publishing, a division of Hachette Book Group, Inc. The Workman name and logo are registered trademarks of Hachette Book Group, Inc.

Design by Becky Terhune

The publisher is not responsible for websites (or their content) that are not owned by the publisher.

Workman books may be purchased in bulk for business, educational, or promotional use. For information, please contact your local bookseller or the Hachette Book Group Special Markets Department at special.markets@hbgusa.com.

Library of Congress Cataloging-in-Publication Data is available.

ISBN 978-1-5235-1807-4

First Edition October 2022

Printed in China on responsibly sourced paper.

10 9 8 7 6 5 4 3